Forward

This booklet was created in an effort to design a reusable basic sociology text affordable to students. I have been teaching the beginning collegiate sociology course since 1991 and continue to find this course to be one of my favorites. I look at the primary purpose of the beginning sociology course to be to provide description and illustration of the terms and concepts common to the sociological discipline. After taking the first collegiate sociology course students should be amply prepared to take additional sociology courses, having an understanding of our basic vocabulary. A second purpose of the introductory course is to provide students with a glimpse of the areas sociologists commonly specialize in.

There are a number of quality introductory textbooks on the market however I find the definitions of common basic terms are not always consistent in these texts. These texts also include a large number of terms I would not consider necessary for the introductory student. In addition these texts typically have current examples and pictures. Examples are important but I feel it is the professor's job to provide relevant, contemporary examples. Including examples in the text requires multiple editions as times change. Removing most of the examples eliminates the need for multiple editions (except when research indicates changing definitions), saving students in introductory courses money. Pictures can be helpful for students to illustrate terms, especially in a media saturated society such as ours. Again, professors can utilize pictures, or even better – ask students to identify pictures illustrating the terms.

The material contained within this booklet has primarily come off of the top of my head. Some of the descriptions may look similar to those found in standard textbooks. This is understandable seeing that I have had the opportunity to utilize a number of different introduction to sociology textbooks over the years including standard ones, classic texts, some unconventional texts, as well as a number of readers. Any similarity to this information is unintentional and reflective of my own developed beliefs about the sociological discipline.

I do hope you find  introduce the
exciting discipline Nov. 2018)

Table of Contents

Basic Terms

Chapter 1   Introducing Sociology

Chapter Purpose
This chapter introduces the discipline of Sociology. It includes the basic definition of sociology, the orientation of sociology, and the three theoretical perspectives in sociology.

Sociology is the study of the social influences on human behavior, attitudes, and feelings. There are three components to this definition – the study, social influences, and human behavior, attitudes, and feelings. To begin, the study of sociology refers to the fact that sociology is a scientific discipline. This means that the scientific method is utilized to come to conclusions about the social influences on human behavior, attitudes, and feelings. The scientific method will be described more completely in Chapter 7 but suffice it to say that the scientific method begins with speculation of what exists and ends with a comparison of that speculation to what is observed in the real world. What is observed in the real world is oftentimes referred to as **empirical reality**. Being grounded in the scientific method allows the sociologist to identify his or her level of certainty in his or her conclusions. Typically, only conclusions with a high level of certainty are identified as fact.

The empirical reality quest in soft or social sciences like sociology begins with speculation. Speculation in sociology is grounded in the scientific orientation a sociologist holds. When scientists speak of **orientations** they are describing what the focus of research is and what is perceived to be the cause of behavior. In the broadest sense there are two possible orientations in the social sciences. One orientation is referred to as a micro-level orientation. A **micro-level orientation** means the researcher focuses on the individual and believes the cause of behavior comes from within the individual. This is also referred to as having an intra-individual focus. Psychology is a micro-level orientation discipline. The other orientation is a **macro-level orientation**. Having a macro-level orientation is also referred to as having an inter-individual focus. With a macro-level orientation the researcher focuses on groups and believes the cause of behavior comes from social influences outside of the individual. Sociologists hold a macro-level orientation.

Sociologists believe that behavior, attitudes, and feelings result from social influences. The size of the group believed to influence behavior is used to differentiate sociologists with those focusing on larger social groups including organizations, as well as the construction of the social structure in general being classified as **macrosociologists** and those focusing on the smaller social groups and how the person's self is formed being classified as **microsociologists**.

Social influences are the second component of the definition of sociology. Sociologists believe that behavior, attitudes, and feelings come about from various social influences. Throughout the course of this booklet the various social influences will become apparent but suffice it to say that social influences include the groups we have belonged to in the past, the groups we currently belong to, as well as the groups we anticipate belonging to in the future. Social influences also include social structural influences such as organizational, societal, and global influences.

The third component of the definition of sociology is human behavior, attitudes, and feelings. Sociology is the study of human phenomena. We focus on why humans act as they do, think as they do, and feel what they do. Sociologists all focus on behavior, attitudes, and feelings. We all hold a macro-level orientation. However, sociological thought within the macro-level orientation can vary depending on what theoretical perspective we come from.

When we are trained as sociologists we are typically trained in one of three theoretical perspectives. A **theoretical perspective** is a belief system about why the world is as it is. The three theoretical perspectives guide a sociologist's theory building and research. The first theoretical perspective is structural functionalism. Structural functionalists are sometimes referred to as functionalists or structuralists. **Structural functionalism** is a theoretical perspective based on the belief that all social structures in existence are present because they fulfill a necessary function for society in order to ensure homeostasis. According to functionalists a **function** is the purpose fulfilled. There are a number of types of functions but the two basic are manifest functions and latent functions. A **manifest function** is the intended purpose the phenomenon fulfills. A **latent function** is an unintended consequence of the phenomenon. Components of the social structure (the phenomena) exist due to the functions they fulfill in order to ensure societal homeostasis. **Homeostasis** refers to balance or equilibrium. Functionalists believe that each part of the social structure is necessary in order to maintain societal balance. If one part of the social structure is modified or changed homeostasis dictates that the rest of the society has to adapt to that change in order to bring the society back to a state of equilibrium.

The second theoretical perspective agrees that parts of the social structure serve functions but argues the functions and homeostasis are not what makes the world tick. **Conflict theory** is a theoretical perspective explaining that the world works based on power differentials. Conflict theorists believe power permeates all relationships. Gaining and maintaining power, according to conflict theorists, is part of small and large group interactions. The structure of relationships is set up to keep those with the power in power and to maintain the subjugation of those without the power all while those without the power continually try to take the power away from those who have it.

The final theoretical perspective would agree that there is structure and there are power differences. However, the **symbolic interactionist** would say, the world runs on the differential meanings different people ascribe to things. Symbolic interactionists believe nothing is inherently real. Reality comes about through the process of negotiation and interaction. What makes something real is not the inherent qualities the person or thing possesses it is the way the thing or person has become defined by the members in a particular society.

Chapter Summary
Sociology is one of the social sciences. The discipline utilizes the scientific method to arrive at its conclusions. Each sociologist will typically align with one of the three theoretical perspectives while holding a macro-level orientation.

Chapter 2   Society

Chapter Purpose
The main topic of sociological study is the concept of society. The numerous types of societies are described in this chapter along with some of their basic characteristics.

Society is the term sociologists use to describe a grouping of people with a boundary governed by a political authority and sharing a dominant culture. If the grouping of people is contained within a larger grouping of people governed by a political authority and sharing a dominant culture the smaller grouping of people is not considered a society. So, a school in the United States (US) is not a society, it is a grouping of people within the US society. The US though is a society. The classification scheme presented in this chapter is the Lenski scheme (Lenski, 1966). The types of societies though are likely to sound familiar. The Lenski scheme is a sociocultural evolutionary theory of how societies progressed from hunting and gathering to post-industrial societies. A **sociocultural evolutionary theory** proposes societies to progress in a set pattern becoming more and more complex and varied. For the Lenski scheme the type of society is based on how the society gathers or obtains resources. The level of technology in the society is what impacts how the society gathers or obtains resources.

The Lenski classification scheme includes six different types of societies each with progressively more advanced technology. **Hunting and gathering societies** are nomadic property-less societies with sustenance gained through foraging. With no personal property hunting and gathering societies typically had limited, if any, inequality. Hunting and gathering societies have the least amount of technology with sticks and rocks primarily being used. As such sustenance was obtained through gathering mostly. Hunting in the earliest hunting and gathering societies typically consisted of hand fishing, throwing rocks, chasing down birds, rabbits, and rats, as well as scaring an animal off a cliff or into water to drown (Leavesley, 2005; Odell, 1988). During the end of the hunting and gathering period society members realized the objects in the environment could be combined resulting in the development of simplistic tools. When the simplistic tools were used to manipulate larger areas of the environment societies changed to horticultural and pastoral societies.

Horticultural and pastoral societies occurred at the same period historically but are different societies. **Horticultural societies** are semi-permanent societies with each family being responsible for its own sustenance through vegetables grown on land they own using rudimentary inventions. Hunting parties were sometimes sent out but for the most part the sustenance came from what was produced. **Pastoral societies** are semi-permanent societies with each family being responsible for its own sustenance using herds cared for on large plots of owned land. Some individual families also planted small gardens but most sustenance was attained through the herds. With the advent of personal property inequality during the horticultural/pastoral period increased. As technological advancement continued the individual rulers of the horticultural/pastoral period obtained more and more land increasing economic surplus. The **agrarian societies** resulted consisting of large-scale permanent societies using large-scale agriculture incorporating inventions and animals to work the land in order to sustain large populations housed in and around cities. Inequality continued to increase along with technology into the next type of society – the industrial society. Subsistence in **industrial societies** came from natural sources obtained through manual labor assisted with the use of human-made machines. Technological advancements continued moving societies into the postindustrial/postmodern type. The **postindustrial/postmodern society** is a large mechanized society with population sustenance coming from natural and synthetic sources manipulated primarily through automated machinery. Work in postindustrial/postmodern societies is primarily service oriented – serving others or servicing machinery, a **service economy**. Postindustrial/postmodern societies typically have more inequality than any other type of society.

Chapter Summary
This chapter provides a description of what a society is as well as the types of societies from a sociological perspective. The classification scheme provided in this chapter utilizes a sociocultural evolutionary theory connecting technology, the economy, and inequality. Using the Lenski scheme six different types of societies have been classified.

References
Lenski, Gerhard. 1966. *Power and Privilege.* New York: McGraw-Hill.

Leavesley, Matthew G. (2005, Spring). "Prehistoric Hunting Strategies in New Ireland, Papua New Guinea: The Evidence of the Cuscus (Phalanger orientalist) Remains from Buang Merabak Cave." *Asian Perspectives,* 44/1, 207-218.

Odell, George H. (1988, June). Addressing prehistoric hunting practices through stone tool analysis. *American Anthropologist,* 90/2, 335-356.

Chapter 3   Culture

Chapter Purpose
This chapter describes the concept of culture along with the four elements used to construct culture. Each element is described along with terms within each element. Also included in this chapter are a few variations related to the concept of culture and concepts impacting how culture is interpreted. The chapter ends with a description of the ways culture changes.

One of the major concepts in sociology is the concept of culture. While there are many different definitions of culture we are going with a very basic definition. **Culture** is the intersection of four basic elements (cognitive, language, material, and normative) constructing both dominant culture and subcultures. The first three elements of culture are relatively straight forward. **Cognitive culture** consists of the beliefs. A **belief** is anything held to be true. Beliefs include those scientifically proven as well as those which have not been, or cannot be, scientifically proven. Beliefs are used to provide meaning to the symbols we use. Symbols are used to construct the second element of culture, language. Communication patterns accepted as appropriate in a society are referred to as **language**. Language includes both verbal and non-verbal communication constructed by those in a society. One theory used in sociology to describe the relationship between language and culture's definition of reality is the Sapir-Whorf hypothesis. The **Sapir-Whorf hypothesis** is a theory indicating the reality in existence is contingent upon the language. Language creates reality. Tangible reality is referred to in sociology as **material culture**. All of the physical things in society make up material culture.

The way beliefs and language are developed and the way one is to use the tangible elements are described by the fourth element of culture, normative culture. The expectations, reinforcement of the expectations, and ideals common in a society defines **normative culture**. Normative culture consists of what the members of society are expected to do, think, and feel. It also consists of how society's members are encouraged to follow those expectations as well as the ideals the expectations are designed to achieve. Normative culture includes three components – norms, sanctions, and values.

Norms consist of the social expectations for behavior, attitudes, and feelings. These are rules set up by society for how we are supposed to act, what ideals and beliefs we are to have, and what we are to feel about things. There are a number of types of norms. The five basic types include **folkways** which are relatively mild expectations with relatively mild negative sanctions for violations and **mores** (pronounced more-ays) which are very strong expectations with severe negative sanctions for violations. Every norm is either a more or a folkway. Every norm also is either informal or formal. **Informal norms** are expectations which are not written down. Written down norms are called **Formal norms**. When formal norms are regulated by the society's political authority figures (the police, military, government) they are referred to as **laws**.

In order to encourage the populace to follow the expectations rewards and punishments are given out. The rewards and punishments designed to encourage appropriate behavior are **sanctions**. When people follow the expectations they are rewarded in various ways when they violate the expectations they are punished. The rewards are referred to as **positive sanctions** while the punishments are called **negative sanctions**. When someone has the job to sanction in a particular way the sanctions they give out are **formal sanctions**. Formal sanctions can be positive or negative, as can informal sanctions. **Informal sanctions** are sanctions given out by informal agents of social control. Essentially, informal sanctions are given out anyone other than formal agents, those who give out formal sanctions. Both formal and informal sanctions can be either positive or negative. The same is true for both internal and external sanctions. **Internal sanctions** are feelings we have when we follow or violate expectations. **External sanctions** are sanctions given out by others or sanctions we give ourselves which originate outside of ourselves. The societal goal is for society's members to internalize expectations. Essentially, it is expected that society's members will internally sanction themselves to follow expectations.

The third component of normative culture is values. They are the organizing feature of society. **Values** are ideals everyone in the society should want to attain. This makes values general. Yet, values are also individual in that each person's definition of a given value varies. Values then are both general and individualized. Other characteristics of values are that they are abstract, positive, and typically stated in one word. Values are connected to the norms which exist in a society. Norms are designed to achieve societal values. The expectations present in a society are present to achieve the values deemed important. Values are also connected to how people view other cultures. The values present impact whether societies' members look at other cultures from the members' own culture or from the other culture's perspective. When people view another culture using their own culture's perspective it is referred to as **ethnocentrism** but when view another culture by that culture's perspective it is called **cultural relativity**. The values present in a society along with the expectations designed to achieve them also influence the response societal members have when confronted with a new culture or subculture (defined below). Ethnocentrism and cultural relativism can lead a person to feel disoriented. The feeling of disorientation which can occur in these situations is known as **culture shock**. Culture shock can be severe leading to a feeling of paralysis or relatively mild leading to a feeling of discomfort.

When the four elements of culture, normative – material – language – and cognitive, intersect in ways considered to be definitive of a particular society it is referred to as the society's **dominant culture**. Because each society has its own dominant culture, culture shock can occur when we are confronted with members from other societies. It can also occur when we are confronted with subcultures different from our own. A **subculture** is a grouping of people who primarily accept the dominant culture and still retain distinct elements. Sometimes the distinct elements though conflict with or contradict elements of the dominant culture. When this occurs the subculture is referred to as a **counterculture**.

Culture can change over time though when it does typically material culture changes faster than the nonmaterial elements. When this occurs the phenomenon is known as **culture lag**. Changes in any of the elements of culture can take place in any of three ways. When two or more things are brought together to create something new an **invention** takes place. **Innovation** occurs when something already in existence is put to new use. And, when something new is found the cultural change called **discovery** takes place.

Chapter Summary
Culture is the product of the four elements of cognitive culture, language, material culture and normative culture. Within normative culture there are five different types of norms designed to achieve

values. As a mechanism to ensure compliance six different types of sanctions can be administered. The intersection of the four elements considered to be mainstream constitutes the society's dominant culture. Variations from the dominant culture results in subcultures as well as countercultures. Contact with dominant cultures, subcultures, and countercultures different from our own can result in culture shock. Our reaction to other cultures, subcultures, and countercultures can consist of ethnocentrism and cultural relativity. Culture can change through inventions, innovations, and discoveries. When cultures change cultural lag can occur.

Chapter 4   Social Structure

Chapter Purpose
This chapter describes where culture is situated, the social structure. What the social structure is included in this chapter as well as the various types of statuses and roles as well as complications which can occur when playing our roles.

The **social structure** provides the framework for social interaction; it is defined as the arena humans are situated in. The social structure is constrained by culture as well as the statuses present in a society. The make-up of the social structure is contingent on the type of society present. The nature of the social structure is limited by the statuses present. A **status** is a position occupied in the social structure. A status is something a person can be. Human is a status but humans is not a status. A person can be a human but cannot be a humans. All of the positions occupied at any one point in time is referred to as the person's **status set.** Each status is classified as either ascribed or achieved. An **ascribed status** is a status one is born with or one the individual has very little control over having. Ascribed statuses are typically not earned. **Achieved statuses** are statuses the person has to do something to get. Both ascribed and achieved statuses can be culturally defined as positive or negative. Both ascribed and achieved statuses can also be master statuses. A **master status** is the overriding status someone uses when interacting with someone else. Master statuses can be relatively stable, shared by many in a society such as one's sex, age, and race. Master statuses can also be specific to an individual's relationship such as a parent using the child status as the overriding status when relating their son or daughter.

Every position occupied in the social structure has expectations associated with it. The expectations for behaviors, attitudes, and feeling corresponding to a particular status are referred to as **roles.** One way to differentiate between statuses and roles is to remember that a person occupies a status and performs a role. All of the expectations for behaviors, attitudes, and feelings associated with a particular status position is called a **role set.** Typically, role sets relate to one status position but it would not be inaccurate to refer to at all the roles associated with a number of statuses occupied as a role set. Following the roles associated with one or more status positions can lead to issues or complications. When there is strain or conflict between the roles of one status position the person is experiencing **role strain**. When the strain and conflict is between the roles of different status positions it is called **role conflict**. When a role associated with a status position is unclear or a person is unsure if he/she is meeting the expectation **role ambiguity** is taking place. Role ambiguity can take place relatively uniformly for all people. When this occurs the role itself is classified as ambiguous. Sometimes though, a role may be ambiguous only for certain people. The person is experiencing role ambiguity though the role itself may not be problematic for all people.

Chapter Summary
The social structure is the place where social interaction takes place. The nature of that interaction is dependent upon the types of statuses and the roles associated with them in addition to culture. A person's status set can incorporate achieved, ascribed, and master statuses. The statuses present in a society are dependent on the type of society the social structure is situated in. The role sets a person performs can lead to a number of complications including role strain, role conflict, and role ambiguity.

Chapter 5   Groups

Chapter Purpose
Groups are an important concept in sociology. The main different types of groups, and non-groups, are described in this chapter. The chapter also includes a glimpse into the decision-making process of small groups.

Sociologists believe that groups serve important functions. Individuals use groups to develop their uniqueness. This process will be explained in the next chapter on socialization. In addition, our behavior, attitudes, and feelings are developed through the groups we belonged to in the past, the groups we currently belong to, and groups we anticipate belonging to. To understand the nature of this important concept it is important to describe what *are* and what *are not* groups. **Groups** consist of two or more people engaged in some sort of interaction. When there is a number of people in close physical proximity but not interacting an **aggregate** forms. Sometimes all of the people with a particular status, such as *students*, is mistakenly referred to as a group. It is not. All of the people sharing a particular status but not interacting with each other is called a **category**.

Groups are classified into a number of types. Groups can be in-groups or out-groups and can be either primary or secondary groups. Sociologists have different definitions of in-groups and out-groups depending on if they are microsociologists or macrosociologists (see Chapter 1 to review this distinction). Starting with the microsociological level, an **in-group at the microsociological level** quite simply is a group a person feels a sense of belonging to and an **out-group at the microsociological level** is a group a person does not feel a sense of belonging to. The in-group/out-group distinction at the macrosociological level is defined based on a person's in-groups at a microsociological level. An **in-group at the macrosociological level** is a group a person's group identifies with but the person does not belong to. An **out-group at the macrosociological level** is a group a person's group does not identify with and the person does not belong to. Groups can also be classified as either primary groups or secondary groups. A **primary group** is a group with relatively concrete boundaries and the group members interact relatively frequently and have intimate knowledge about each other. **Secondary groups** are groups with relatively fluid boundaries and the group members typically interact with each other in a patterned manner resulting in general knowledge about each other. Primary groups are typically smaller than secondary groups.

One of the larger groups sociologists study is formal organizations. **Formal organizations** are large secondary groups deliberately and rationally planned to achieve a specific goal. Formal organizations can be organized using a number of different organizational processes. A bureaucracy is one technique for organizing formal organizations. A **bureaucracy** is an organizational process utilizing a division of labor, specialization, authority hierarchies, impersonality, and formal written rules and regulations. Formal organizations can also be organized using collegial associations. A **collegial association** is an organizational technique where the formal organization members are considered to be colleagues, each with different areas of expertise but none better than another. A third organizational structure is a **collectivist organization** where the formal organization members are not bound by rationale organizational techniques and frequently share jobs as well as authority.

Whether a group is small or large, decisions have to be made. Sociologists identify a number of processes related to groups making decisions. One process is conformity. **Conformity** is a change in behavior or belief toward a group as a result of real or imagined group pressure. Conformity can take a number of forms. The first form is **conformity without authority** where a person conforms when there is no one directing him/her to do so and/or there is no potential reward or punishment from an authority figure for doing so. Another form conformity takes is **conformity to authority** where a person conforms because an authority figure requires it. A third form of conformity can occur in conjunction with the other two. It is conformity to role expectations. **Conformity to role expectations** occurs when people conform to the expectations for the role for a status position occupied. Another group decision making process is groupthink. **Groupthink** is the term for the process where a group makes a poor decision due to no discussion based on the belief that each member knows what each other member is thinking. Another group decision making process is known as polarization. **Polarization** happens when a group's decision is more extreme than the individual members' decisions. In order for polarization to happen the group must engage in true discussion. **True discussion** occurs when each every group member's opinion and knowledge level are considered important and used to arrive at a decision. A second condition necessary for polarization is that the group has to be homogeneous. **Homogeneity** is the term used for a group of people similar on basic social characteristics.

Chapter Summary
Groups are the hallmark of the sociological enterprise. Groups are different from aggregates and categories and can be in-groups, out-groups, primary groups, or secondary groups. Groups can also be formal organizations organized through bureaucracies, collegial associations, or collectivist organizations. When groups make decisions conformity, groupthink, or polarization can occur.

Chapter 6   Socialization

Chapter Purpose
This chapter provides a description of socialization and the socialization process. The chapter concludes with an explanation of some of the features related to socialization.

The preceding chapters provided a description of what societies consist of, what culture and the social structure are, and how they construct the way we act, think, and feel. The last chapter provided a description of various groups which also impact our actions, thoughts, and feelings along with helping to form our identity. The sociological concept of socialization helps to explain how all of this takes place. **Socialization** is the term used to describe the process of learning who we are and how to behave, think, and feel in the society we are situated in. Sociologists use the concept of the **self** to describe the unique identity of an individual. The self is formed through a series of interactions which can be broadly summed up with the looking-glass self theory. Charles Horton Cooley's (1902) **looking-glass self** posits the self is formed through a three step process where (1) we imagine the self, (2) we imagine others' reactions to the imagined self, and (3) based on what we think others think we modify or maintain the self. The others who help shape our identities, those who socialize us, are referred to as **agents of socialization**. Agents of socialization can be people as well as non-people. Agents of socialization can be of one of two types. **Primary agents of socialization** are the agents with the most influence over us. **Secondary agents of socialization** have influence over us but if that influence contradicts a primary agent of socialization the secondary agent's influence is reduced or eliminated. A couple of additional characteristics of the socialization process include whether we are engaging in anticipatory socialization or being resocialized. **Anticipatory socialization** occurs when an individual practices playing a role prior to taking on the status position and being expected to play the roles associated with that status position. **Resocialization** is the re-teaching of who we are and how we are to behave, think, and feel. Resocialization happens after an individual has already been socialized and was socialized inadequately for some reason. Resocialization can be relatively mild and inconsequential. It can also be extensive, essentially modifying (or attempting to modify) the entire self. Extensive resocialization can take place in a total institution. A **total institution** is an organization designed with the primary purpose of resocialization. Total institutions typically have barriers designed to limit the movement of those being resocialized. The process of socialization is complex reflecting the symbiotic relationship between the self and society.

Chapter Summary
This chapter described the manner in which the individual and society itself is formed. Both are formed through the process of socialization incorporating various agents of socialization, using in part, the looking-glass self theory. Individuals in society can engage in anticipatory socialization as well as be resocialized in total institutions.

Chapter 7   Sociological Research

Chapter Purpose
The final chapter introducing the discipline of sociology describes the manner in which sociologists obtain their information. The chapter describes the major components of the scientific method.

As social scientists many sociologists conduct research on a regular basis. All sociologists earning a masters degree or above (and some bachelors programs) are trained on how to conduct social science research. There are a number of steps to conducting research. The steps social scientists use are the same as those used in the hard sciences. The difference between the sciences comes with the nature of some of the steps. The first step when conducting research is to develop or choose a research topic and create a research question. After that the researcher conducts a literature review. A **literature review** is an exhaustive review of academic theories and studies on the topic selected. From the literature review the variables and hypothesis of the study are designed. A **variable** is anything with more than one attribute or subcategory. A **hypothesis** is a specific statement about the relationship between two or more variables. Every hypothesis will have at least one independent and one dependent variable. The **independent variable** is the variable thought to or known to lead to change in another variable. The **dependent variable** is the variable expected to be changed or modified by the existence of a particular attribute of the independent variable. After the construction of the hypothesis the variables are operationally defined. An **operational definition** is a description of an abstract concept specific enough to be measured. The literature review guides the operational definitions just as it guides hypothesis construction.

Once hypotheses are developed the sociologist begins the data collection process. Before data are collected though the researcher has to consider the rights of their subjects and the type of study to conduct. This is one of the differences between the hard and soft sciences. When humans are used as subjects there are a number of rights they have. First, humans have the right to informed consent. **Informed consent** means subjects have the right to be told the general nature of the study and be given the opportunity to consent to participate in the study. Second, human subjects also have the **right** to **privacy** where human subjects have the right to know that their names will not be connected with the data provided either through an anonymous or confidential study. In an **anonymous study** the researcher cannot connect subjects' names to their data while in a **confidential study** the research can connect the subjects' names to their data but promises not to do so. The final right of human subjects is the **protection from harm** where subjects have the right to not be harmed physically, mentally, or socially through participation in the study, unless if it is for society's good. In addition to the rights of their subjects, researchers also have to consider the type of study to conduct. The type of study is based on what the data to be obtained will look like. In **quantitative studies** the data take numeric form and in **qualitative studies** the data do not take numeric form.

Once the rights of human subjects and what the data will look like are taken into consideration the researcher then decides on the **research method or design** which is the procedure for gathering data. There are a number of possible research methods or designs. A **survey** which is a series of questions given to subjects to elicit opinions can be conducted. An experiment is another possibility. An **experiment** is the creation of an artificial environment involving the manipulation of one variable (the independent) to assess its impact on another variable (the dependent). In an experiment the researcher controls on all other possible variables and places subjects into an experimental or a control group. In an **experimental group** the subjects are given the independent variable variation. The **control group** consists of those subjects not given the independent variable variation. A researcher may also choose to conduct an **observational field study** defined as watching people in their natural setting. Observational field studies can vary based on researcher participation and subject awareness. When the researcher joins the group being studied it is referred to as a **participant observational field study** and when he/she does not join the group being studied it is a **nonparticipant observational field study**. **Overt observational field studies** occur when a leader of a group and/or those being studied know they are being studied. When subjects are not aware they are being watched it is called a **covert observational field study**. A researcher could also use secondary analysis to gather data. **Secondary analysis** is the use of data already in existence. Content analysis is another option for gathering data. **Content analysis** is analyzing a form of communication. Content analysis can be conducted within context or out-of-context. In a **within context content analysis study** the meaning of the form of communication is relevant and in an **out-of-context content analysis study** the meaning of the form of communication is not relevant. A final option for the researcher is triangulation. **Triangulation** is the use of two or more research methods/designs to gather data. Once a method/design has been chosen the step becomes complete through using the design to gather the data.

Once the data are gathered the researcher then has to analyze the data in order to assess the accuracy of the hypothesis. When the study is a qualitative study data analysis takes the form of looking for themes and patterns in the data. When the study is quantitative data analysis is done through the use of statistics. A **statistic** is a number that results from a mathematical equation that summarizes data. There are a number of statistics sociologists can incorporate when analyzing data. Two statistics which form the basis of most statistical analyses are measures of central tendency and correlations. A **measure of central tendency** is an average. Three averages include the mean, median, and mode. The **mean** is the mathematical average, the **median** is the exact middle number in a numeric array placed in order, and the **mode** is the most frequently occurring number. A **correlation** is a statistic that indicates the nature and strength of the relationship between two variables.

The purpose of evaluating the accuracy of the hypothesis provides another distinction between soft and hard sciences. With hard sciences the purpose is to confirm causality. Soft sciences cannot confirm causality because we cannot conduct true experiments. In a **true experiment** the researcher is able to control on every other possible variable than the independent and dependent variable. In the hard sciences the hypothesis can be proven. In the social sciences hypotheses can only have support. As such, in the social sciences the researcher looks for relationships or patterns.

The final step in the scientific method is to report study results. Researchers have two basic options for reporting the results of a study. First, the researcher can present at a professional conference. In this format, the researcher gives a brief presentation of the study and study results. Then the researcher fields questions by other experts in the study topic. The second way to present results is in the form of an empirical article. Empirical articles are also sometimes referred to as professional journals. They are peer-reviewed. This means that the decision to publish is made by other experts in the study topic.

Chapter Summary
This final chapter in the basic terms series provided a glimpse into the scientific method utilized by sociologists and other scientists. The scientific method steps from topic choice, literature review, hypotheses development, research design, data analyses, and presentation of study results were described.

Sociological Subdisciplines

Now that the basic terms and concepts have been described as well as the basics of sociological research, now we get into the areas sociologists specialize in. Each of the following chapters describe a particular area of specialty. I refer to these as the sociological subdisicplines because each specialty area incorporates the basic terms and concepts putting them into use for a particular problem or topic. The following chapters include a description of the basic characteristics of each subdiscipline as well as some general topics typically studied.

Chapter 8   Deviance

Chapter Purpose

This chapter introduces the first sociological subdiscipline. It includes the basic description of deviance and how deviance is defined and dealt with. The four classic theories of deviance are introduced and various types of deviance are also explored.

One of the areas sociologists can specialize in is the study of **deviance,** the violation of a norm. What is defined as deviant depends on who is doing the defining and for what reason. Due to the relative nature of deviance it is important to understand the various ways deviance can be defined. Six of the *Ways of Establishing Deviance* include the **statistical/numerical view** which says that deviance occurs when a numerical minority engage in the behavior. The second way of establishing deviance is the legal statute view. The **legal statute view** defines deviance as anything against the law. Another way of deciding what is and is not deviant is through the moral view. The **moral view** indicates that deviance occurs when a moral code is violated. The moral view is similar to the **sinful view** of deviance which indicates deviance occurs when a sin is violated. Another way of establishing deviance is based on how the person feels. If the person feels guilt he or she is deviant using the **self view.** A final way of establishing deviance is through the use of the **consequence view** of deviance. This way indicates deviance occurs when there are negative effects of the act on others.

The ways of establishing deviance demonstrate the relative nature of deviance in that a particular behavior, attitude, or belief could be classified as deviant by one way and normative by another. Once deviance has been established it can generally be classified into one of six different types. **Crime** – the violation of a law – is one type of deviance. Another type of deviance is substance use. **Substance Use** is the use or abuse of a chemical substance capable of altering the mind. Substance use can include prescriptions, over-the-counter medications, supplements, and illegal substances. **Mental illness** is a form of deviance where an individual is defined by society as exhibiting unusual or inappropriate behavior, attitudes, and/or feelings. When an individual engages in sexual practices conflicting with those indicated as appropriate by the dominant culture **sexual variance** takes place. **Institutional deviance** occurs when a formal organization reinforces or requires practices considered inappropriate by dominant cultural standards. Institutional deviance includes deviance perpetrated by or within formal organizations including governments. The final type of deviance is commonly referred to as everyday deviance. **Everyday deviance** is essentially everyday activities, thoughts, or attitudes found to be deviant. Everyday deviance is typically deviance that does not fall within any of the other types of deviance and can include things such as getting tattoos, piercings, picking one's nose, and swearing in public.

People then are classified as deviant in a number of ways and can fall into a number of types. The question then becomes why people are deviant. Sociologists do not believe deviance comes from within so all sociological theories of deviance will explain how the social structure leads to deviance. While there are many theories of deviance four basic ones are described here. The first theory is Merton's structural strain theory (1938). This theory is also referred to as Merton's anomie theory. Deviance based on **structural strain theory** develops when an individual is confronted with a situation where he or she cannot, or chooses not to, desire socially approved goals and/or cannot, or chooses not to, follow socially approved means to achieve those goals. Instead of focusing on the impact of the larger social structure, differential association theory (Sutherland, 1939) focuses on interactions with society's members. **Differential association theory** indicates deviance forms through interaction with deviant others who are part of the individual's primary group. Control theory (Hirschi, 1969), the next theory, brings both the larger social structure and the connection an individual has to it into play. Using **control theory,** deviance results when an individual is not connected to society and hence society is unable to its controls on the individual. The last theory brings together a number of symbolic interactionist theorists' ideas (Blumer, 1969; Goffman, 1963; Schur, 1971). In a nutshell, **labeling theory** indicates deviance results from the designation of a person as deviant.

When someone engages in deviance society's members respond by attempting to bring the deviant person back in line through the use of negative sanctions. When punishing a deviant there are various motivations behind the punishments. These motivations are referred to as *Views of Punishment*. There are four views of punishments with one view having two variations. The first view of punishment is retribution. **Retribution** is subjecting the offender to suffering comparable to the offense committed. A second view of punishment is **social protection** where the offender is rendered incapable of committing the offense through expulsion, extermination, or incarceration. **Deterrence** occurs when a potential offender is threated to thwart additional offenses. Deterrence has two variations. In **specific deterrence** the offender is threatened with punishment but is not actually punished. The idea behind specific deterrence is to make a person who committed a deviant act too scared to commit that same act of deviance again. General deterrence occurs when the threat is to others, not the offender. Here the offender is actually punished. The offender is punished as an example of what will happen to others who commit the act. Through using the offender as an example **general deterrence** threatens those who have not committed the act. The idea here is that others will be too afraid to do what the offender did due to what happened to the offender. The final view of punishment seeks to resocialize the offender. Resocialization of the offender is **rehabilitation**.

Chapter Summary
The study of deviance is one sociological subdiscipline. This chapter describes the nature of deviance, the techniques used to define deviance and the subsequent types of deviance. Also included in the chapter is four basic theories explaining why people are deviant and the punishment motivations used on those considered deviant.

References
Blumer, Herbert. 1969. *Symbolic Interactionism*. Englewood Cliffs, NJ: Prentice-Hall.
Goffman, Erving. 1963. *Stigma: Notes on the Management of Spoiled Identity*. Englewood Cliffs, NJ: Prentice-Hall.
Hirschi, Travis, 1969. *Causes of Delinquency*. Berkeley: University of California Press.
Merton, Robert. 1938. "Social Structure and Anomie". *American Sociological Review* 3:672-682.
Schur, Edwin M. 1971. *Labeling Deviant Behavior: Its Sociological Implications*. New York: Harper & Row.
Sutherland, Edwin H. 1939. *Principles of Criminology*. 3rd ed. Philadelphia: Lippincott.

Chapter 9   Social Stratification

Chapter Purpose

Chapter 9 provides the basic terms and concepts in the sociological subdiscipline of social stratification. The chapter begins with a description of the basic terms necessary to understand the basis of this subdiscipline. In addition the chapter provides a description of the seven basic systems of stratification in the United States as well as the patterns of majority/minority relations.

Social stratification is a broad subdiscipline which explores the ways in which societies get segmented. **Social stratification** is the structured ranking of individuals in accordance with the number of desired qualities a person possesses. Essentially social stratification is the classification of people into ranked categories based on the desirability of characteristics possessed. Where a particular person falls within the ranking depends on whether the characteristics a person is perceived to have are "good" or "bad" characteristics. Where a person falls in the ranking system impacts whether the individual has advantages or disadvantages in the quest for wealth, power, and prestige. In order to maintain the systems in place prejudicial thoughts and discriminatory practices are developed and encouraged.

      Prejudice is an irrational attitude about a category of people. Prejudice can be positive or negative and cannot be eliminated through logical thought. Prejudice is always based on eliminating the individuality of a person, instead looking at a person as representative of an entire category of people. Prejudice is a thought. Discrimination is a behavior. **Discrimination** is differential treatment of a category of people. Discrimination, like prejudice, can be positive or negative. When discrimination is positive it provides a category of people an advantage. When it is negative it provides a category of people a disadvantage. Discrimination, like prejudice, is based on placing people into categories, again eliminating the person's individuality. Prejudice and discrimination typically go together but they do not have to. Merton (1957) provided a classification scheme of the various ways prejudice and discrimination can relate. Merton's scheme is based on whether the person is or is not prejudice and whether the person does or does not discriminate. The scheme results in four categories, the **active bigot**

who is prejudice and does discriminate, the **timid bigot** who is prejudice but does not discriminate, the **fair-weather liberal** who is not prejudice but discriminates, and the **all-weather liberal** who is not prejudice and does not discriminate.

Prejudice and discrimination are the basis for the systems of stratification which exist in a society. When a series of prejudicial thoughts are brought together to come to a prejudicial conclusion about a category of people it is classified as an **ideology**. When multiple ideologies are brought together to justify differential treatment (i.e. discrimination) it is referred to as an **ism.** The isms form the systems of stratification. In the United States some of the most common systems of stratification include classism, racism, sexism, ageism, heterosexism, lookism, and ableism. Each ism is created based on the category of focus. Though the definitions may appear redundant they are included here.

Classism is a series of ideologies used to justify differential treatment based on social class.

Racism is a series of ideologies used to justify differential treatment based on race.

Sexism is a series of ideologies used to justify differential treatment based on sex.

Ageism is a series of ideologies used to justify differential treatment based on age.

Heterosexism is a series of ideologies used to justify differential treatment based on sexual orientation.

Lookism is a series of ideologies used to justify differential treatment based on cultural notions of attractiveness.

Ableism is a series of ideologies used to justify differential treatment based on physical and/or mental ability.

The designation of people into desirable or undesirable categories impacts the way society members relate to people through providing advantages or disadvantages in the attainment of wealth, power, and prestige. The classification of people then forms the basis of the patterns of majority/minority group relations.

What is considered to be a majority or minority group is based on the system of stratification, though some could argue they can be defined for the entire society. A **majority group** is the category of people who possess the dominant culturally defined desirable quality within a system of stratification. The majority group is afforded advantages designed to maintain their high strata position.

The **minority group** is the category of people who possess the dominant culturally defined undesirable quality. Minority group members have disadvantages imposed on them to ensure their low strata position is maintained. The patterns identifying how majority and minority groups interact with each other has also been classified. When it is expected that the minority group give up their subcultural characteristics and take on those of the majority group it is referred to as **assimilation**. **Multiculturalism** is the existence and acceptance of multiple categories with their distinct subcultural qualities within a society. When multiculturalism exists there can still be a majority group and a minority group but the majority group will typically have less power than in societies with other majority/minority relationship patterns. When members of the majority and minority group interbreed, essentially creating a new "combined" group it is referred to as **Amalgamation.** While it is appropriate to talk about most of patterns of majority/minority group relations for all stratification groupings, amalgamation is typically discussed mainly when referring to racial classifications. Amalgamation is more likely to be accepted in multicultural societies than in societies employing assimilation or segregation. **Segregation** occurs when the majority and minority groups are separated from each other. One possible consequence of segregation is the attempt to eradicate a minority group, a process known as **genocide**.

Chapter Summary
Some sociologists specialize in the study of the groupings of individuals into categories which are subsequently provided with more or less access to wealth, power, and prestige. This specialty is social stratification. This chapter provided the basic terms in stratification literature and the basic patterns used by majority and minority groups when relating to each other.

References
Merton, Robert. 1957. *Social Theory and Social Structure.* New York: Free Press.

Chapter 10 Collective Behavior and Social Movements

Chapter Purpose
In this chapter the sociological study of collectivities is described. Both crowd and mass collectivities are included in the description along with Smelser's (1962) conditions for collective behavior. The chapter ends with a basic description of social movements.

Evaluating very large numbers of people interested in the same person, event, or idea is quite interesting. Some sociologists specialize in such study. Large in this case is defined as more than 50 people. When a large number of people are focused on a particular person, event, or idea it is referred to as a **collectivity**. Collectivities can create either crowds or mass behavior. **Collective behavior** refers to either crowd or mass behavior engaged in my collectivities. **Crowds** are collectivities in close physical proximity. There are a number of different types of crowds. First, crowds can be either casual or conventional. A **casual crowd** is a collectivity which spontaneously forms whereas a **conventional crowd** is a planned collectivity. Either a casual or conventional crowd can become an expressive crowd. Not all casual crowds or conventional crowds become expressive crowds. When they do though it is emotionally charged. So, an **expressive crowd** is an emotionally charged crowd. Some expressive crowds become acting crowd. An **acting crowd** is a crowd that engages in violence and/or destruction. Acting crowds are also sub-classified into three types. First, an acting crowd can be a riot. A **riot** is a spontaneously formed acting crowd with no leader orchestrating the entire event. **Mobs**, the second type of acting crowd looks like a riot but it is typically planned and has clear leadership. A **panic**, like a riot and mob, engages in violence and/or destruction but does so due to a perceived threat. A final type of crowd is a protest crowd. **Protest crowds** are collectivities forming to elicit social change.

Crowds then are collectivities in close physical proximity. **Mass behavior** occurs when collectivities are not in class physical proximity. Just as there are a number of types of crowds there are also a number of types of mass behavior. The types of mass behavior are not each connected to each other as is the case for much crowd behavior. One type of mass behavior is a fad. A **fad** is mass behavior where there is relatively short-lived wild enthusiasm about a particular person, event, or idea. Generally also existing over a limited time period is mass hysteria. **Mass hysteria** is mass behavior utilizing an irrational response to a perceived threat. Mass hysteria can look like a panic but over a wide geographic area. Rumors are another short-lived mass behavior. **Rumors** are unsubstantiated stories spread through a wide geographic area, usually by informal means. If a rumor does withstand the test of time they may turn into legends. Legends are also sometimes referred to as folklore. A **legend** is mass behavior consisting of an unsubstantiated story more durable than a rumor typically spread informally usually with several local variations. Some legends are **traditional legends** which are based on events beyond the perceived natural world commonly supernatural in origin. **Urban legends** are those based on mysterious human behavior or including mysteries of the natural world. Urban legends often depict clashes between modern conditions and some aspect of traditional life.

Whether one is looking at crowd behavior or mass behavior, Smelser's (1962) theory of collective behavior provides one description of how any form of collective behavior emerges. Smelser's theory posits six determinants of collective behavior development. The determinants or conditions have been regarded as going in order. The first condition is structural conduciveness. **Structural conduciveness** means that the necessary conditions exist for a form of collective behavior to emerge. Second, **structural strain** described as societal tension occurs. The third condition is the generalized belief. The **generalized belief** is the labeling of the tension from the second condition. Collective behavior next requires a **precipitating incident**, the event leading directly into mobilization. While there are typically a number of precipitating factors, the precipitating incident is described as "the straw that breaks the camel's back." **Mobilization**, the fifth condition brings together the collectivity. The final condition is the breakdown of social control. The **breakdown of social control** occurs when normal social control mechanisms which would have stopped the collective behavior from emerging are absent or ineffective.

Collective behavior can exist in its own right. Collective behavior can also be part of social movements. **Social movements** are formalized activities by collectivities to bring about social change. Social institutions are formalized in that typically formal organizations emerge connected to the attempted social change.

Aberle (1966) described how social movements vary based on the focus of change. Social movements can be identified based on the breadth and depth of change desired. The breadth of change indicates how wide the change goes. Is the social movement attempting to small groupings of people or is the focus on the entire society? The depth of change indicates how deep of change is desired. Is the social movement attempting to elicit smaller types of change or entire change? Using this classification scheme four types of social movements emerge. **Alternative social movements** seek limited breadth and depth of change. **Redemptive social movements** seek limited breadth and complete depth of change. **Reformative social movements** look for a wide breadth but limited depth of change. The final type of social movement is the revolutionary social movement. **Revolutionary social movements** seek a wide breadth and complete breadth of change.

Chapter Summary
The subdiscipline of collective behavior and social movements focuses on very large numbers of people. Sometimes these people are in close proximity and other times they are spread across a wide geographical area. The different types of crowds and different types mass behavior are described in this chapter as are the various types of social movements.

References

Aberle, David F. 1966. *The Peyote Religion among the Navaho.* Chicago: Aldine.
Smelser, Neil J. 1962. *Theory of Collective Behaviour.* Abingdon, Oxon UK: Routledge.

Chapter 11   Demography

Chapter Purpose
Demography focuses on the study of population patterns. The various patterns are described as are population pyramids. Models designed to explain how cities emerge are also described.

Demography is the study of population characteristics and patterns. Demography is typically split up into population studies and urbanization. Population studies focus on population patterns. A number of rates are necessary to understand population patterns. The **birth rate** is the number of babies born to women of childbearing age per 1,000 women. The **death rate** is the number of people who die per 1,000 people. **Replacement level fertility** in a society occurs when two children are born for each mating couple. **Below replacement level fertility** occurs when less than two children are born for each mating couple. **Immigration** refers to the number of people coming into a geographic area. **Emigration** is the number of people leaving a geographic area. One way to see various population characteristics is through the use of population pyramids. A **population pyramid** is a pictorial representation of a society by age and sex. Typically, males are on the left of the pyramid and females are on the right. Age is then segmented in five or 10 year increments.

Population development may lead to the emergence of urban areas. The study of urbanization includes a review of the ways cities emerge. **Urbanization** itself is defined as the process by which large cities supporting dense populations are developed. Three basic models have been developed to describe how urban areas emerge. Each model begins with three basic components – business, finance, and government. Each model also describes the typical pattern of residence by social class.   In the **concentric zone model** business, finance, and government are all located in a small central geographic area followed by residence patterns and then agriculture. Community residence surrounds the central area in a circular manner resulting in a bullseye look to the urban area. Lower class residences surround the central area, middle class after that, and upper class surround the middle class. Surrounding all the residences is agriculture. In the **sector model** the central area sounds or straddles a waterway or railway with residence patterns coming out of each in wedges. The pie-shaped wedges typically begin with the lower class residences followed by the middle class in a larger area, the upper class taking over even more area, and then agriculture. The final model is the multiple-nuclei model. In the **multiple-nuclei model** the central area is spread out with residences shooting out of each part of the central area in either a concentric zone or wedge pattern.

Chapter Summary
The study of population patterns and urbanization make up the study of demography. This chapter provided a description of the various terms which make up the study of population. Finally, the chapter described the three models of how cities, urban centers, emerge.

Chapter 12   Sexuality

Chapter Purpose
The sociological perspective on sexuality is provided in this chapter. The chapter begins with the definition of sexuality and sexual scripts. It continues with the discussion of a few of the sexuality cultural universals. The chapter concludes with a review of a few of the cultural differences in sexuality with a description of the perspectives on sexual intercourse and the sexual standards.

Another subdiscipline sociologists can specialize in is the study of sexuality. The study of sexuality begins with a common understanding of what sexuality is. **Sexuality** is the feelings and drives, as well as the sexual practices common to a society. The social construction of these feelings, drives, and sexual practices becomes apparent through the concept of sexual scripts. A **sexual script** is the social expectations for sexual behavior, attitudes, and feelings (Gagnon & Simon, 1973). Sexual scripts identify three important components of sexuality, the actors, the interactions, and the context.

There appears to be three cultural universals regarding sexuality. A **cultural universal** is a trait found in all cultures. The first cultural universal is the incest taboo. An **incest taboo** is a prohibition of sexual intercourse with certain family members. A second cultural universal is marriage. Marriage exists in all cultures. Who is included in a marriage though varies from culture to culture. The final cultural universal is heterosexuality as a norm. Heterosexuality is the norm but homosexuality is always present.

Along with cultural universals there are also sexual differences among and between cultures in thoughts about the appropriateness of sexual acts among various segments of society. There are various perspectives on sexual intercourse. These perspectives indicate what the purpose of sexual intercourse in among married heterosexual couples. First, there's the procreational perspective. The **procreational perspective** indicates that the only legitimate reason for sexual intercourse is to produce children. The **relational perspective** indicates the only reason for marital sexual intercourse is to enhance a relationships. The final perspective on sexual intercourse is the recreational perspective. The **recreational perspective** indicates the only reason to for a marital couple to engage in sexual intercourse is for enjoyment. Standards also have been developed for the non-married. The sexual standards indicate when it is appropriate for non-married persons to engage in sexual activity. There are five sexual standards. First there is the **abstinence standard** which indicates that sexual activity outside of marriage is forbidden. Next, there are the double standards. The first double standard is the **traditional or orthodox double standard** which indicates sexual activity outside of marriage is always ok for males and never ok for females. The **transitional double standard** also indicates sexual activity outside of marriage is always ok for the males; sexual activity outside of marriage is ok for females when they are in a committed relationship. If the female is not in a committed relationship sexual activity outside of marriage is not ok. The last two sexual standards do not base the permissiveness on a person's sex. The **permissiveness with affection** standard indicates sexual activity outside of marriage is always ok as long as the people involved care for each other. The final sexual standard is the permissiveness without affection standard. The **permissiveness without affection standard** indicates sexual activity outside of marriage is always ok, even the people involved do not care for each other.

Chapter Summary
The sociology of sexuality incorporates the study of the nature of sexuality, sexual scripts, cultural universals, and cultural differences. Three basic cultural universals were explored as well as cultural differences. Cultural differences included differences in perspectives on sexual intercourse and sexual standards.
Reference:
Gagnon, John. H. and William Simon. 1973. *Sexual Conduct: The Social Origins of Human Sexuality*. Chicago: Aldine.

Chapter 13   Social Institutions

Chapter Purpose
This final chapter describes the nature of social institutions. Included in the description are the five core institutions necessary for all societies. Included as well in the chapter is a description of the additional three social institutions present in industrial societies and beyond. The description of each social institution includes some of the basic terms within each institution.

All sociologist incorporate the study of social institutions in their specialties. Some sociologists also have a particular social institution or parts of a social institution as their specialty. All sociologists specialize in the study of social institutions in some way or another in part due to the nature of social institutions in general. Social institutions are the backbone of society. They are what make up a society. A **social institution** is a stable cluster of norms, values, roles, and statuses centered on the fulfillment of social needs. In order for a society to exist there are a number of needs which must be met. Social institutions provide the social structure necessary to meet those societal needs. This chapter focuses on the terms specifically oriented around the fulfillment of the social needs within each social institution. Some social needs are present in all societies, such as the replacement of society's members and the provision of the physical health of the population. Core institutions emerged to fulfill these common needs. The core institutions are present in all societies. Over the years as societies advanced a number of additional needs emerged. As necessary societies developed additional social institutions to meet these additional needs.

Core Institutions
There are five core institutions. Again, a core institution is present in all societies. One core institution is the family institution. The **family institution** is a stable cluster of norms, values, roles, and statuses centered on fulfilling the societal needs of population reproduction, sexual regulation, belongingness, primary group protection, and the informal transmission of culture.   While there are a number of aspects concerning the family institution subdiscipline this chapter focuses on marriage. **Marriage** is defined as a publically recognized union between two or more people where they are united

sexually, cooperate economically, and may give birth to, adopt, or rear children. Within marriage there are a number of factors including contracts, marriage styles, and residence patterns. When people marry they are expected to follow the marriage contracts. Two marriage contracts are present in all societies and one is present in societies with laws (see chapter 3 for a reminder of the definition of a law). The first marriage contract is the social contract. The **social contract** is made up of the societal roles of married couples. The **legal contract** consists of all the laws those married are expected to follow in terms of marriage and family life. The final contract is the **individual contract** made up of the marriage participants' individual expectations for their marital roles. Marriage can consist of a number of styles. These styles were developed based on heterosexual marriages. As of yet, homosexual marriages have not been classified using these styles. **Monogamy** occurs when one man marries one woman. **Polygamy** exists when one person of one sex marries multiple people of the other sex. Polygamy takes two forms, **polygyny** where one man marries multiple women and **polyandry** where one woman marries multiple men. **Group marriage** occurs when a multiple people are married to multiple other people. All of the members are jointly married to each other. The final style of marriage is **cenogamy** where everyone in the society marries everyone else. When people get married they can conform to one of three residence patterns. The newly married can live with or near the groom's father. The groom's father makes family decisions. This residence pattern is called **patrilocal**. In a **matrilocal residence pattern** the newly married life with or near the wife's mother and the wife's mother makes family decisions. Finally, the newly married can participate in a **neolocal residence pattern** where the newly married establish their own residence away from their parents.

The second core institution is the religious institution. The **religious institution** is the norms values, roles, and statuses designed to fulfill the societal needs of explanation of the world, provision of peace, and explanation of why we are here. A **religion** is defined as socially agreed upon beliefs and rituals oriented around the sacred. That which is **sacred** is that which is awe inspiring. The **profane** is the term used for things which are ordinary. There are a number of ways to classify religion. Two such schemes include one based on belief system and one based on structure. The types of religion based on belief system classifies religion based on beliefs about what is considered to be sacred. In **theism** the sacred is defined as one or more supernatural beings. There are two theistic religions, monotheism and polytheism. **Monotheism** is the belief in one supernatural being. **Polytheism** is the belief in more than one supernatural being. In **ethicalism** the sacred is defined as moral principles for living and in **animism** the sacred is defined as anthropomorphized spirts which are part of the natural world. The classification scheme based on structure includes four types. The first type of religion based on structure is an ecclesia. An **ecclesia** is a national religion. The second type is a denomination. A **denomination** is a mainstream religion accepting the notion of religious pluralism. **Religious pluralism** is the belief that there are multiple legitimate religions. A religious **sect** does not accept the notion of religious pluralism, comes from a denomination, and uses conversion techniques to recruit new members. A religious **cult** also does not accept religious pluralism and uses conversation techniques to recruit new members along with being based on new or unusual beliefs.

Another core institution is the **political institution** – the norms, values, roles, and statuses designed to fulfill the societal needs of provision of social order/structure and the distribution of power for the maintenance of social control to protect society's members. The political institution is based on the distribution of power. **Power** is the ability to make someone do something he or she does not want to do. There are two types of power, authority and coercion. **Authority** is legitimate power. Authority can take a number of forms. **Traditional authority** is authority based on custom or tradition primarily incorporating both achieved and ascribed statuses but focusing on ascription. **Charismatic authority** is authority based on having qualities conducive to having people follow, based primarily on ascribed statuses. The final type of authority is **legal-rational authority** which is based on achieved statuses with roles typically specified by written rules and regulations. With authority the people subject to the power accept that the person has to right to make them do something. With **coercion**, which is illegitimate power, the people subject to the power do not accept that the person has the right to make them do something. Because coercive power is not accepted as legitimate those attempting to use coercive power have to use threats of force or actual force to ensure compliance. Types of power impacts the form of government in a society. A **government** is an individual or group with total control of the society's social institutions. There are a number of types of government; four basic ones follow. An **autocracy/monarchy** occurs when a single person has total control of the social institutions. An **oligarchy/aristocracy** exists when a small group of people have total control of the social institutions. The third form of government is totalitarianism. **Totalitarianism** is defined as a formal organization with total control of the social institutions. Totalitarian regimes typically have heavy-handed control of the social institutions. The final form of government covered in this chapter is a democracy. A **democracy** exists when a formal organization has total control of the social institutions and civilian rule, and public liberties, and a representative government. **Civilian rule** means every citizen has the right to be elected into office. **Public liberties** are inalienable rights – rights the government promises to not take away. A **representative government** exists when those elected into office make decisions based on what their constituents want rather than the government official's own desires.

The fourth out of five core institutions is the economic institution. The **economic institution** consists of the norms, values, roles, and statuses designed to fulfill the societal needs of the gathering and distribution of resources and beginning in the horticultural/pastoral period the development of property for the establishment of inequality. Three basic economic systems exist within the economic institution. An **economy** is defined as the way resources are gathered and distributed. One economic system is capitalism. **Capitalism** exists when private individuals and/or corporations own the means of production. The **means of production** essentially is another word for the economy. The second economic system is **socialism** where the government owns the means of production. Most societies though are not purely capitalist or socialist. Most societies have a **mixed economy** containing some socialism and some capitalism. The relationship between socialism and capitalism to the forms of government creates what are referred to as political economic systems. There are a number of possible classifications here but we're going to focus on those based on totalitarianism and democracies. In a **democratic capitalist** political-economic system the government is democratic and the economic system is capitalism. In **democratic socialism**, the form of government again is democratic but this time the economic system is socialist. **Fascism** exists when totalitarianism is combined with capitalism and **communism** exists when totalitarianism is combined with socialism.

The final social institution present in all societies is the health institution. The **health institution** is made up the norms, values, roles, and statuses designed to fulfill the societal needs of the maintenance of the physical, mental, and social health of the population along with the need for the gatekeeping of medicinal remedies. The health institution is all about the health of the population with **health** being defined as a relative state of physical, mental, and social well-being. We know there is a relationship between a person's physical, mental, and social health in that each impacts the others. When a person is not in a healthy state there are particular expectations placed on the unhealthy person which are referred to as the **sick role**. We also know that health is connected to the social structure. In hunting and gathering societies, for example, health issues are perceived to be caused by some sort of defilement from the environment of other people. Treatment of health issues in hunting and gathering societies primarily takes the form of ritualistic cleansing. In horticultural and pastoral societies illness is perceived to be the result of contagion from illnesses others have. Treatment in horticultural and pastoral societies focuses on various herbals designed to cleanse the person and attempts at eliminating exposure to the infected. In agrarian societies, contagion continues to be the perceived cause including contagion from unclean spirits. At this point, historically, societies also became aware of the impact of population density on health. Treatment of illness in agrarian societies included herbal combinations and attempts to cleanse the life-force or blood of the human body through exorcisms, blood-letting, and leeching. Movement into the industrial period brought the rise and acceptance of the medical profession and the medicalization of society. The **medicalization of society** is the process by which the domain of medicine is extended to areas of life previously referred to as non-medical. Illness becomes thought of as originating both inside and outside of the person. Treatments focus primarily on modifying the ill through medication and surgeries. Movement into the post-industrial/post-modern period brings even greater emphasis on the physical state of the individual more so than the other two forms of health (mental and social) into the diagnosis and treatment of illness.

Non-Core Institutions

The final three social institutions developed as societies became more technologically advanced and new social needs emerged. A new social institution emerged with each new type of society. In the horticultural/pastoral period a new need emerged leading to the development of the education institution. The **education institution** is the norms, values, roles, and statuses centered on fulfilling the societal need of the formal transmission of culture and, after the agrarian period, reading, writing, and logic instruction along with the transmission of job skills. A few additional terms clarifies the nature of the education institution. There is a difference between learning and education. **Learning** is defined as socialization, both formal and informal. **Education** is defined as formal socialization within institutions other than the family. The **curriculum** is what is taught in the education institution and how it is assessed. The **hidden curriculum** is what is taught implicitly in the education institution through curriculum material, school formal rules and regulations, school activities, and informal school norms.

As societies advanced into the agrarian period the work institution emerged due to the development of additional social needs. The **work institution** is the norms, values, roles, and statuses centered on meeting the societal needs of identity markers to reach adult goals, the acquisition of money to obtain resources, and to justify the education institution. The work institution emerged as the definition of work changed. **Work as an individual activity** is the goal expenditure of energy with an intrinsic value, defining the person in his or her totality. In agrarian societies work became defined as a structural activity. **Work as a structural activity** is the socioeconomic process of commodity/service production used to satisfy societal needs. It was in the agrarian period that occupations developed. An **occupation** is a job requiring specialized training. A consequence of defining work as a structural activity is alienation. **Alienation** is the disassociation of one's labor from the product, process, self, and others. There are four types of alienation. **Alienation from the product** is the disassociation of one's labor from the object produced or service provided. **Alienation from the process** is the disassociation of one's labor from how the product or service is produced. **Alienation from the self** is the disassociation of one's labor from one's identity; it's the fragmentation of identity.

The final type of alienation is alienation from others. **Alienation from others** is the disassociation of one's labor from those consuming the product or service as well as co-workers and those assisting in the production of the product or service.

The final social institution recognized as emerging emerged in the industrial period. The **entertainment institution** is the norms, values, roles, and statuses designed to meet the social needs of mass communication, time occupation, relaxation, and eventually the explanation of reality. Most of the information about the entertainment institution comes from a postmodernist theoretical framework. **Postmodernism** is a theoretical framework critical of the effects of technology on society in general and individuals specifically. One of the social needs necessitating the emergence of the entertainment institution led to the development of mass communication. **Mass communication** consists of various communication techniques designed to disseminate information to a large, spread out, populace. The norms, values, roles, and statuses within the entertainment institution are recognized as existing in two formats, sport and mass media. **Sport** has been defined by Edwards (1973) as activities having formally recorded histories and traditions stressing physical exertion through competition within limits set in explicit and formal rules governing role and position relationships carried out by actors who represent or who are part of formally organized associations having the goal of achieving valued tangibles or intangibles through defeating opposing groups. The second format the entertainment institution is played out in is the mass media. The **mass media** is the medium present through which mass communication takes place. The mass media began as **auditory messages** consisting of music and orally transmitted stories. Gradually the mass media transitioned into the **written word**, language on paper and then into the **visual image**, a pictorial or symbolic representation of an object or concept. The mass media typically incorporates subliminal messages in symbols and in hidden meanings. A **subliminal message** is a form of communication masked by the manifest form of communication not attended to by the conscious mind but having an impact on the recipients' thoughts and/or behaviors.

Chapter Summary
Social institutions are the staple of societies. They are designed to fulfill social needs and include both core institutions and non-core institutions. The core institutions are the family, religious, political, economic, and health institutions. The non-core institutions include the education, work, and entertainment institutions. The chapter provided basic definitions of each institution as well as definitions of various parts within each social institution.

Reference:
Edwards, Harry. 1973. *Sociology of Sport.* Homewood, IL: Dorsey.